Tyler Noah David • David´s Reflections on the Love of Animals

Tyler Noah David

David's Reflections
on the Love of Animals

FOUQUÉ PUBLISHERS NEW YORK

Copyright ©2011 by Fouqué Publishers New York
Originally published as *Davids Betrachtungen über Tierliebe, 2010*
by August von Goethe Literaturverlag

First American Edition
Printed on acid-free paper

Library of Congress Cataloging-in-Publication Data
David, Tyler Noah
[David´s Reflections on the Love of Animals / Tyler Noah David]
1st American ed.

ISBN 978-0-578-09465-6

Table of Contents

Foreword

The sign of true humanity is that one recognizes the rights of everyone, not just of oneself, to develop to their full potential. Above all, this applies to the weakest among us: our pets. If I deprive the weakest among us of their natural-born rights, then I no longer have the right to call myself an animal lover.

I am writing this book because that is MY point of view on this subject, and I would like to share my point of view with other people. I do not expect that this will also become YOUR opinion. Everyone sees things from their own perspective, and that is good and that is how it should remain. But nevertheless a book like this should make one think, and if as a result of this thinking someone's opinion is changed just a tiny little bit, no one will think anything of it; you can even deny that you read this book, you can even say that your little change of heart was your own idea.

But if as a result of whatever may happen, just a few animals in this world suffer less, then this book will have fulfilled its purpose!

The soul of an animal is just as gentle and fragile as the soul of a human being.

In the civilized world, where human beings have subjugated nature, they have the responsibility of protecting such a sensitive soul.

2. Never Torment an Animal For Fun, Because They Feel Just Like We Do! (*Quäle nie zum Spaß ein Tier, denn es fühlt genau wie wir!*)

This is an old German proverb. We will be referring to it a lot, because it contains a fundamental truth:

Animals feel just like we do. And only when we try to put ourselves in their place can we understand how our animals feel. Self-proclaimed animal experts can say what they will, but nobody can even begin to understand how a cat feels after it has been neutered. As long as we continue to rationalize and look down on them and invent excuses (oh, they don't feel a thing, etc.), we will never be able to relieve the suffering of animals. Only when we elevate the event to our level and picture how WE would feel if someone did that to US, then and only then are we truly able to relate to it. When things happen to others and when we DON'T put ourselves in their place, we quickly tend to say, "he shouldn't carry on so." Once we put ourselves in their place, we will then be able to open up our hearts and empathize because the same thing could happen, or perhaps already has happened, to us.

An example: according to statistics, 60% of Germans cheat on their spouses. Most of them don't think anything of it, because they don't put themselves in the other's place. When he gets caught, he wonders why she's making such a fuss. "Good Lord, it didn't mean a thing, it was only physical, I had a bit too much to drink, couldn't control myself, blah! blah! blah!" But when she goes and does the same thing and he catches her, he lets loose! "You hussy!" Now he is wounded to the very depths of his soul and claims he will never be able to forget it for the rest of his life. If he is told, "But you were unfaithful yourself," he will probably respond, "That was different."

However, if before he cheated he had first closed his eyes and taken time to think and reflect: "How would I feel if my wife cheated on me?", then I don't believe he would ever have been capable of cheating because now he knows how it feels when it happens to him. And that is exactly what one should do before one oppresses, locks up, or maims another creature.

3. What Is "The Love of Animals"?

There are some people who claim that they are animal lovers simply because they own an animal. But if that were so, then the slaveholder in ancient Rome would have been a true friend of human beings because he owned some. Others think of themselves as animal lovers because once in their lives they fed a duck in a pond, and there are still others who claim to be animal lovers because they don't own a fur coat. But by the same reasoning, a bum on a park bench could just as easily claim that he is very environmentally conscious because he doesn't drive a car.

And there are some smart-alecs out there who claim to be animal lovers because they like steak or fried chicken.

But what is "the love of animals" really? Have you ever truly thought about it?

Well, at least it contains the word "love."

If one looks for definitions, one will find a wide variety. But basically the world is in agreement that love is unselfish. In other words, if I only love someone because he can give me this or that, then that is not true love, that is only calculating and egotistical, everyone agrees on that. "She's just a gold digger," is what one would say about a woman like that.

In wisdom teachings one finds that true love is a love that only gives without wanting to take. That could be interpreted to mean that if I truly love a person or an animal, my sole interest is that person's or animal's well-being, that he/she/it is happy, regardless of whether or not I approve of his/her/its behavior or whether I benefit from his/her/its existence.

At this point one should ask oneself if a self-proclaimed animal lover ever acted out of these noble motives when he acquired his pet.

At this point I would like to state emphatically that in the vast majority of cases, animal owners in Germany acquire animals because they are thinking about what THEY want, what THEY are getting out of it. HIS or HER motives come first; whether or not that would make the animal happy never enters into it. What the animal needs or doesn't need they got out of books that were written by human beings, or they simply accepted what they heard or what Uncle John or whoever told them, assuming they even gave it any thought in the first place. Deciding what truly makes the animal happy means finding out how the animal lives in the wild: not how the animal can live well in captivity, but how well it lives in the wild! If someone wants to find out what makes another person happy, he doesn't look at it from the perspective of a prison warden, who reflects on how a person in custody can survive in a reasonably humane manner. That would be completely idiotic. [That's like saying] I want to find myself a wife and I'm thinking of how I can confine her to the kitchen and to the bedroom. That would be warped and my fellow human beings - at least the female ones - would treat me with contempt.

Take the wild rabbit, for example. It is a very social animal that lives in colonies or warrens consisting of a series of underground tunnels. Obviously they love their freedom and reproduce, which can be viewed as the purpose of life for all living creatures.

So when I buy a dwarf rabbit and put it in a cage by itself, however big this cage may be, then this animal is not being kept in a species-appropriate manner. There it sits, alone for most of the day, slowly but surely becoming lonely and going nuts. If I truly wanted to keep it in a species-appropriate manner, I should provide it with an environment where it could burrow and reproduce in the company of others of its kind.

Is confining the rabbit in a cage generally no bigger than a square meter [3 square feet] for the rest of its life love of animals? Lifelong solitary confinement in an extremely small space. And without a court decision! If that happened to a human being, the whole world would be in an uproar. If a person who loves animals wanted to raise rabbits, then he would have a yard in which he could fence off a certain section in which to keep several rabbits. He could build them a stall, but one which they could leave and go out into "their" yard whenever they wanted. There they could dig, have a place to run, and reproduce. How many people are willing to do all of that for their rabbits? But it is precisely those few animal owners who are true animal lovers. If I cannot provide that for an animal, then I should not get one. That would be no different than a woman who lived under a bridge wanting to have a child, but knowing full well that she cannot give that child what "normal" children can expect as a matter of course. Doing something like that would be called reckless [reckless endangerment of a child].

At this point I would like to make the admittedly very bold statement that most people who are animal lovers do not own any animals. It is not my intention to criticize or condemn those who do, but I would like every animal owner to consider that perhaps their animal deserves a much better lot in life.

4. Why Do People Have Pets?

Nature never intended for different species of animals to keep company with each other. Has anyone ever seen a deer and a squirrel living together out in the wild? Or a hedgehog befriending a jackrabbit? That only happens in fables. Nature is very clear on this. Different species of animals are just too different, even those like the deer and the jackrabbit that wouldn't devour each other, to be able to interact with each other. They lack the means to communicate sufficiently with each other. For that reason different species of animals ignore each other, unless they are natural enemies. Anything else is something imposed by humans, and is neither in the interest of nature nor other animals. Any relationship between humans and animals is based on compulsion, which originates with humans (although in a few isolated cases - such as crab lice - this compulsion originates with the animal). At this point many will say, "But I didn't force my hamster to do anything!" Yes you did! You bought him and took him with you, you are at least 1000 times heavier and stronger than him, and you gave him no chance to escape. Indeed you did compel him. Anyone who owns an animal compelled the latter to be with them. Measures were taken to deprive that animal of freedom. The animal really has no other choice but to cooperate with you or die. Hence its natural survival instinct unconsciously compels it to come to terms with you. Psychologists refer to this behavior as "Stockholm Syndrome". Any animal that lives isolated from its own kind in a household suffers from this syndrome. It could not survive otherwise.

It all started with livestock thousands of years ago. People and their livestock used to share the same living quarters so that the animals wouldn't freeze to death in winter. Today there are still underdeveloped regions where people share living quarters with their chickens. And obviously the farmer needed a cat to keep the mice under control, a watchdog to warn of intruders, and a horse for transportation. The bad habit of keeping animals in apartments gradually evolved out of this practice. But those are behavior patterns of people of bygone ages. Back then people NEEDED those animals because they had jobs that the humans themselves weren't able to do. Cars, mouse traps, and burglar alarms hadn't been invented yet. But nowadays? Who needs a cat in his apartment nowadays to keep mice under control? The Flodders [dysfunctional family in a series of Dutch comedy films] maybe, but who else? These behavior patterns are completely antiquated, but they mean much suffering for our animals.

Admittedly there are a great many different motives for why people get animals; obviously there are people who simply like animals, no one will deny that, but usually there are other reasons behind the animal purchase. And even if the person simply likes the animal, could it be possible that the animal may not like that person?

We experience the same thing when looking for a spouse; just because I really like a particular woman, that certainly doesn't mean that the woman also likes me. And [although] we all want to find a boss who pays well and offers a good working environment, [it doesn't necessarily work that way]. The animal is sold like a commodity and must now make the best of its lot in life. Why then do people have animals?

It starts with Grandma, whose husband has passed away and who buys a poodle or German Spitz to keep her company and to have something to look after. As a general rule the dog is also a better listener than Grandpa ever was. Normally these "little old ladies' dogs" don't have such a bad life, in contrast to ones whose owners work. Unless Grandma too were to go to the green pastures and Fido has to go the pound.

Others buy a dog because Uncle John told them that walking a dog is a good way to meet someone. But after taking the dog out for the umpteenth time and running into nothing but bothersome neighbors that one would rather avoid, it becomes obvious that Fido hasn't fulfilled his purpose. One then goes looking for love elsewhere, and Fido becomes a bothersome chore. Still others get a dog in order to get some exercise themselves. But because such good intentions generally have very short half-lives, the dog walks gradually get shorter and shorter and more routine. Then there are some who seek to define themselves through their dogs. They get a fighting dog so that they can boast, "I've got a Pitbull." Often the dog is supposed to give the master a strength that he himself lacks. Obviously the real reason for having the dog is to make up for the owner's inferiority complex; the dog's welfare is of but secondary importance. Others buy a dog simply because they grew up having one: "It's normal to have a dog." Thus the animal is acquired because having a pet is what a person is expected to do. For me it is hard to see any true love of animals in these cases.

And then there are the total failures, who otherwise don't have a lot of say in life. At work it's "David do this, David do that." He is at the bottom of the chain of command. Then at home it's "Tyler take out the trash, Tyler do this, Tyler do that. Not TONIGHT, Tyler, I've got a headache."

The bottom of the pecking order ... unable to stick up for himself... but he can get a dog, and now things will change!! "Sit here!! Go there!!" The dog is the only being in the entire universe who looks up to him in awe. Obviously he is no better off than before, but now he has someone else to take his frustrations out on and he is glad that he was not born a dog. Then there are countless children who want a pet and who generally neglect it completely. In most cases the chore of taking care of the dog falls to the parents who often go about it indifferently; no one feels truly responsible. Taking care of the animal is a continuous source of contention, and obviously the animal bears the full brunt of it. The numbers of animals abandoned every year and the numbers in the pound speak volumes! Imagine how you would feel if you had to pee so badly that you could hardly hold it in any longer, and mother and son just stood there arguing who is going to take you out. That is barbaric! That is torture!

Many people, women in particular, buy a cat because they do not want to be alone. They are thus exploiting the animal because they are not capable of finding a decent partner. The woman is now no longer alone, but the cat is, at least for most of the day. Somehow that seems rather ironic. I'm lonely, therefore I'm going to get a pet, lock it up, and now this animal is lonely. But somehow, someday, she meets Mr. Right - at any rate she thinks he is - and the cat then spends the rest of its life in the pound.

What I am really driving at is this:

The reason for getting a pet, whatever it may be, is neither here nor there. In principle it's about the person and his motives; rarely does one ever think about the animal.

A small animal with a sensitive soul is completely helpless in the hands of a strange, stronger being, and has no rights! The desires and preferences of the animal are ignored, as are its innate behavior patterns and instincts.

It is always interesting to note what kind of people buy which pets. It is often possible to judge by the dog what complexes his master has.

Then we have those situations with a high embarrassment factor, such as seeing a man of Helmut Kohl's stature walking a miniature pinscher or how often dog and master look astonishingly alike.

5. Animals: "Man's Best Friend"?

Far from it, I'd say. The only friend, perhaps, if you could call him that. The best friend perhaps, if I look at just one side of the whole matter. A person who has no friends because he has no social skills may get a pet and call it his best friend. Let's say a woman buys a guinea pig so that she has some company. She comes home, feeds her guinea pig, and gushes over it. In contrast to a person, this small guinea pig won't tell her she's talking nothing but utter nonsense, but instead it will respond to her words with a squeak at the most, which Mommy naturally immediately interprets as agreement. "At least you understand me, Petey."

Obviously "Petey" is far from doing so. "Petey" doesn't even know far away from home who he really is. He only has vague memories of other guinea pigs from the pet store. Little "Petey" lives in the most secure maximum security prison in the world. The security at Alcatraz was like an old ladies' rest home by comparison. The cage in which he lives is nearly impregnable. But even if he were able to get out, the next hurdle would be the apartment. Even if "Petey" were to muster all of his gray matter and trick Mommy into leaving the apartment, he would still have to get out of the building. And what then? The small guinea pig would find himself in a very hostile environment. He could never survive the winter, nor would he find other guinea pigs out in the wild. "Petey" would have to seek out an airport or seaport and stowaway on a plane or a ship in order to get back to his South American home. And do so with no money and no passport. To put it briefly, there is no way that "Petey" can escape this life that was forced upon him. Best friend? Not hardly. They always look so sweet on packages of pet food, and one could believe that the animal is happy. But that is what advertising is all about:

you always get told what you want to hear, or what will make you buy something. They even manage to make a milk snack for children with more than 30% sugar and 26% fat seem light and healthy, even if they have to buy Germany's most beloved boxers to do so.

Would one lock up one's best friend??

Let him be castrated??

Give him nothing but canned food to eat??

Ignore his wishes??

Lock him in a small cage where he is forced to eat and sleep a mere 30 cm [12 inches] away from his own feces??

Force him to pose??

Deny him contact with his own kind??

How dare anyone say that his pet is his friend? The animal is merely his prisoner.

6. Do Animal Lovers Truly Love Animals?

We have actually already answered this question above. But nearly all animal owners think they are animal lovers. But they don't have the foggiest idea what love of animals even is, let alone what such an animal needs most of all, namely its freedom! They cannot and do not want to see that the animal is suffering. If the dog is happy when Master comes home, that is a sign that the dog has it darn good. And if he also has a shiny coat like in the advertisements, then there can be no doubt that he is a truly happy dog. But when you take him out, why then does Fido tug hard on his leash as soon as he sees another dog? When was the last time that your dog actually had any contact with another dog? And I'm not talking about ten seconds of sniffing before he is yanked away, but true contact, perhaps an hour of playing with another dog? Or sex? 99% of all pets die without ever having had sex. And that's not because they voluntarily took a vow of celibacy, it is because they simply weren't allowed to do so! They die as virgins! What if you were in solitary confinement, with strange beings, would you be happy? If you were even halfway sociable, not hardly. Then what makes you think your dog is happy, if you would not be, in the same situation? I think the truth of the matter is that you would rather not think about it. Deep down in your heart it makes no difference to you whether or not your dog is happy, all that matters is how you feel. What if someone asked you how you would feel if someone locked you up and cut off your testicles, like you did to your cat? You would probably say "that's different." Of course it's different, because it wasn't YOUR testicles that were cut off! I don't know about you, but I'd defend my testicles with my life! But we're just talking about a small helpless cat that can't fight back. When you say "but that's different," what you're really saying is that it never occurred to you that this is a living thing with a purpose in life and a soul. For you it is merely a toy, a means to satisfy your ends, a commodity. Even veterinarians say things like this. And that is not surprising, after all they earn good money because people have pets. When a veterinarian says, "The cat won't feel a thing," he means that purely from an anatomical standpoint. But were we to do the opposite experiment and cut off Mr. Veterinarian's testicles, he wouldn't feel a thing either if it were done professionally and under anesthesia. Then he gets a few pills to dull the pain afterwards and everything's fine! But what happens to the creature afterwards, whether veterinarian or tomcat, is devastating. Doc Veterinarian would probably succumb to the greatest crisis in his life. His hormone balance would collapse, and life would no longer have any meaning. When a veterinarian says something like that (but the cat won't feel a thing), you'd think you were talking to a car mechanic doing an oil change. The German Federal Code for Veterinarians (Bundes-Tierärzteordnung) states:

§ 1

The calling of the veterinarian is to prevent, alleviate, and heal animal suffering and animal diseases.

Let me repeat that: to **prevent** suffering!

There is nothing in the code that says he should simply castrate the animal merely because Mommy wants it that way. But after all [the cat's] Mistress is paying for it, and if he doesn't do it, somebody else will. So he accepts the blood money, for what does it matter to him whether or not some cat loses his testicles, after all he still has his! And when the veterinarian tells Mistress that the cat won't feel a thing, she, in awe of his white coat, takes his word as law. But that's all the same to him; he knows, or should know, what he is really doing.

And that is precisely what's wrong, that hardly anyone cares how the little animal feels; they are only interested in themselves. The breeder needs his income, as does the veterinarian, and you need a cat because otherwise you'd be lonely. And the veterinarian's job is to ensure that the cat is calmer and does not smell so badly. What's wrong is that most animals are only castrated to make them more manageable. But who can the cat mate with, when he's in solitary confinement anyway? It is really terrible that the animal protection law allows that. Hello, you legislators, we're talking about an animal PROTECTION law here. Like the word says, it is there to protect animals. Nevertheless animals by the millions have their genitals amputated just because it gets on Master's nerves when the cat gets randy and YOU gave your OK for it, you should be ashamed to keep calling it an animal protection law...! All that this subsection of Paragraph 6 does is allow people to mutilate animals without being punished for it, just so that they have less work managing these animals. People need to understand that we are talking about one of nature's creatures here, for which you cannot simply buy an accessory like you can for a car. I can't park? OK, let's add a parking assistance system. You don't like the smell? OK, one castration please, that will be $150. And you have become so accustomed to this that you probably no longer realize what a cruel, egotistical behavior this is. If something like this bothers you, you shouldn't get an animal; buy a stuffed animal or a Tamagotchi instead. And the veterinarian? Although he mutilates animals everyday just because Mistress wants it that way, he still feels that he is a true Christian. The word castrate comes from the Latin castratus, and stands for steal, take away, debilitate, weaken. That alone says that we are not doing something good to the animal. The side effects range from a tendency to obesity, loss of drive, depression, and hormonal instability to metabolic disorders. Speaking purely hypothetically:

I would bet that if they rounded up young men and made them decide, and gave them no other alternatives, whether they preferred having their ears cropped so that they looked like Mr. Spock or castration, 100% of the young men would go home with Spock ears. The ironic thing is that cropping a dog's ears is forbidden; it is considered mutilation. Obviously that's how it should be, but compared to loss of masculinity this procedure seems harmless. So if ear cropping is torture and mutilation, how is it that you can allow castration? §6 of the Animal Protection Law prohibits the amputation of body parts in animals. Obviously an exception is made for the gonads, although castration assuredly does the most harm of all to a living creature. But it all comes down to our **convenience**. After all it isn't reasonable to expect people to have an intact animal and a little more work to do because of it.

Obviously you only want the best for your pet. I'm sure that you don't want to hear any of this. You just want everything to stay the same and David should just shut his trap and has no business inciting pets to turn on their masters or to make animal owners feel guilty. But that's exactly the way some macho men thought many years ago, in the early days of the women's rights movement. "Just keep your traps shut, you fool women's libbers, before my wife gets dumb ideas of her own. After all, I like things just the way they are." Well, obviously it was nice for him that he could indulge himself as he pleased and his wife served him. Admittedly, I can understand where you're coming from to some extent, along comes this idiot named David and tells you you're not being fair to your pet. Obviously you don't like that, but you can't stop progress either. Victor Hugo once said, "Nothing is more powerful than an idea whose time has come," and I feel certain that humankind will become more democratic when it comes to raising animals as well. Why should it be otherwise? Just because a dog can't mark a ballot? Neither can a child. Just because a dog isn't truly capable of rational thought and acts more on instinct? A baby doesn't do any differently. Because a dog has no buying power? Neither does a baby. But just like babies, dogs too feel sorrow and pain and loneliness. Every creature has a sense of pain, and just because an animal is smaller doesn't mean it feels less pain, any more than a big animal feels more pain. Why is it OK to make a slave out of a horse but not a human being? Why do we talk about human rights when we as humans suppress and maim other creatures and see that as perfectly normal? Because the animal cannot defend itself? We are simply the stronger ones and that's that. We keep animals as living toys; after all they are much more entertaining than Barbie and her friends. But where is our conscience? Where is our sense of justice? Taking an animal, mutilating it, locking it up for life with no contact with its own kind. For what? Because that's just the way we are? So that I'm not alone? Good Lord, then go to a bar if you don't want to be alone, take up sports or visit a museum, or whatever else strikes your fancy, but don't torture an animal because of it.

7. Would I Do This To a Human Being?

Now let's ask ourselves a very specific question: What if I did to a person what happens to animals, what is DONE to animals, done by US to them every day? Not because my survival depended on it, nor because I had no other choice, but just for fun? Let's think through a brief scenario: a middle-aged nurse, let's call her Hilde, just went through a divorce. She's now relieved, but also lonely. She decides to go to Africa to fetch a small boy. She gets him from the poorest region of the poorest country. A boy with a 95% probability of dying had she not gotten him. She secretly smuggles this boy back to her home. There Hilde gives him a place to sleep, feeds him, gives him toys, and talks to him in a language he doesn't understand. Nor is he supposed to understand her. All he's supposed to do is LISTEN. If he did understand her, he would eventually put his own two cents' worth in or else tell her she's talking crap. No, she doesn't want that at all, that's all she's ever heard, his opinion is of no interest whatsoever, she doesn't want to communicate, just talk. Unload her mental baggage somewhere. Obviously the apartment will be secured so that the boy cannot get out. Because she heard somewhere that young colored boys start to smell when they reach puberty, she cuts off his testicles to be on the safe side. And why not? He will never need them anyway! Why should she burden him with having urges that he can't satisfy, not to mention making stains in her clean, sterile apartment; that would be unacceptable. After all the boy should be grateful that she took him in everyday he can eat his fill and his survival is ensured. That he must make a few adjustments himself is certainly not too much to ask! By the time the little boy is a 25 year old eunuch, he will undoubtedly have become resigned to his fate and in some ways even find his life bearable. He has gotten used to sitting when told, every day he gets a can of ravioli, sometimes with meat in the sauce, sometimes not, sometimes with pork, sometimes with beef. Hilde heard that that is the ideal nourishment for blacks and also that they only need one meal a day. Besides it is also quite cheap, after all she's just a nurse and not a doctor. If he begs while she is eating, she shoves him away with the words "That's not good for you," (which he obviously doesn't understand) and she points with her finger to his can of ravioli. He has his toys, all he wants to eat, Mommy sometimes pats him on the head when she gets home. There he sits, a young man, who once had goals and desires, who wanted to make something of himself, start a family, have children, defend his property, and fight for those whom he loves. But there he sits, a shadow of what he could have become. In my opinion death would be a blessing for him.

Let us now assume that a neighbor were to find out and alert the police. The young man, now 30, would undoubtedly have to spend the rest of his life in some kind of home, because he couldn't make it on his own. In court Hilde would insist over and over again that he didn't feel a thing when he was castrated, after all she put him to sleep and gave him pills to stop the pain afterwards. And she only did it because it was best for him. All she ever wanted was the best for him, she would insist with tears in her eyes. But did she really? Or was she only thinking of herself? When she says she only wanted what was best for HIM, that's a lie. She only wanted what was best for her! Obviously if you keep lying to yourself over and over again, eventually you will actually believe it. But everyone is supposed to have an innate sense of right and wrong. And taking a creature and locking it up, mutilating it, and forcing it to live a life that it **never** would have willingly chosen is injustice that cries out to heaven. Any child with a sound sense of justice knows this. But evidently there are no limits to egotism.

Even if his chances of survival in his homeland weren't the best, he still had a chance to do something great, to live, to love, and to realize his own potential.

In August of 2009 I read in the news that a woman in Texas castrated her five week old son. That was two years ago, but the trial was going on now. The judges sentenced her to 99 years in jail. This is a clear statement that cutting someone's testicles off is **not** a trivial offense. The harsh sentence was justified by the fact that she condemned her son to a horrible life. He will have to take hormones for the rest of his life and will require lifelong medical care. Obviously we don't do that for our beloved pets. Where would we be if they constantly needed hormones? Who'd pay for it? Whether the cat even still knows whether its male or female, whether it gets depressed, or gains weight (just give it less to eat) makes absolutely no difference to us, the only thing that matters is that our apartment stays clean and that we don't have so much work.

One really can't say how the judges in Germany would rule. The charge would be kidnapping, deprivation of liberty, severe bodily injury, maiming.

This woman would either go to jail for a very long time or be put in a padded cell. But even with that, she could never make up for having robbed this person of his life, his entire identity.

But when people do the exact same thing to a little tomcat and are then called animal lovers, that should really make us stop and think long and hard.

8. What Is Animal Cruelty?

Excerpt from the German Animal Protection Act:

§17

Whoever:

1. kills a vertebrate animal without a legitimate reason or

2. through brutal actions, causes a vertebrate animal

a) severe pain or suffering

or

b) longer-term or recurring severe pain or suffering

shall be sentenced to up to three years imprisonment or fined.

I would submit that considerable suffering is inflicted on any animal kept in captivity in a confined space. If they kept you in solitary confinement for life, with no judgment, wouldn't you perceive that as longer-lasting or recurring suffering? I sure would. And the fact that this is considerable suffering is true around the world, otherwise deprivation of liberty wouldn't be a punishment. Therefore whatever makes some people think that it makes no difference to their pets to be locked up?

Quäle nie zum Spaß ein Tier, denn es fühlt genau wie wir [German proverb: "Never torment animals for fun, because they feel just like we do."].

Then why do we lock them up for life if we ourselves consider it to be an ***extremely harsh punishment***? No, it is not different! Even if we do not choose solitary confinement when, for example, we buy two rabbits, that doesn't mean by a long shot that the animals are now better off, because even animals choose whom they wish to be with. What if you were condemned to life-long imprisonment and they locked you up in a small cell with a total moron? You would beg for solitary confinement! Human rights organizations worldwide condemn solitary confinement. So it's OK for us to do that every day to millions of our pets? For the pet owner yes, but certainly not for the animal. The German Animal Protection Law also makes provision for the species-appropriate keeping of animals:

Whoever keeps, cares for, or is in charge of caring for an animal:

1. must provide the animal with species-appropriate and needs-appropriate food and care, and behaviorally-appropriate housing;

2. must not limit the animal's opportunity for species-appropriate movement in such a way that causes it pain or unnecessary suffering or harm;

3. must possess the knowledge and capabilities required to provide the animal with proper nourishment, care, and behaviorally-appropriate housing.

The species-appropriate feeding of an animal is not even possible in the case of predators. A predator, if you please, likes to catch and kill its own lunch. What if you, who from a zoological standpoint are an omnivore, were given a live chicken to eat? You would sit in your cell with your chicken and it would be a question of who dies first. If you die first the chicken would feed on you, but most likely not the other way around. I'm willing to bet that the probability that you would starve would be extremely high.

Anyone who thinks about "...behaviorally-appropriate housing" would have to come to the conclusion that this paragraph alone should suffice to ban all animal keeping at once. I would state flat out that all animals being kept in apartments are not being housed in a behaviorally-appropriate manner. In the wild wolves and cats have their own territories that must also be marked, rabbits burrow, birds fly. I think it is especially bad to keep birds in cages in which they can't fly. And usually they spend their said existence all alone. In the wild parakeets live together in large flocks, frequently as many as several hundred birds in complete freedom. Dear animal rights activists, why don't you push for a ban on keeping birds in such a cruel manner? Would you consider it species-appropriate if they kept you in a cage in which you couldn't walk? Is it species-appropriate housing when a dog doesn't have a place to go to the bathroom? Toilet deprivation is considered internationally as a method of torture! If you google the term "toilet deprivation," you will find numerous articles stating that this method violates the Basic Law, the Penal Code, and Article 3 of the European Convention on Human Rights. Abuse, bodily injury, and duress are mentioned. But this happens to nearly all dogs in Germany every day, and you see that as completely normal. If your son in school were not allowed to go to the bathroom during class, you would probably call your lawyer, yet you do this to your dog every day.

Once I logged into a forum for dog lovers, and the toilet topic came up for discussion. As I read it, I noted that not even dog owners who have a yard allow their dog to relieve itself in it. Could someone please tell me what's up with that? A pile left in their yard by their oh-so-beloved dog is just too much for the masters. So they go out and let him poop on the sidewalk where someone else can step in it instead. If you really stop to think about, such audacity and laziness is quite shocking. Such behavior is just plain socially unacceptable. That is truly living at the expense of others. It gives true meaning to the words "überall liegt Scheiße, man muss eigentlich schweben" ["there is crap everywhere, you have to float to avoid it"] in a song about Berlin by Peter Fox.

Imagine that someone meets a woman, loves her very much (he says), and wants her to live with him so that he's not alone. But she should go to the bathroom someplace else, if you please, because he doesn't particularly like the smell. Well, lots of luck! I'm afraid a guy like that will die an old bachelor. But your dog doesn't even need to be asked, he is simply forbidden to relieve himself inside and that's that! As a test such people should be sentenced to toilet deprivation and then they can see for themselves that it's no piece of cake to have to hold it in for ten hours.

9. Can You Imagine?

Imagine that you were born somewhere and while you were still a child some big, strong, strange beings came and took you away. Let us use a Tyrannosaurus rex as our imaginary example. An immense, powerful, and totally alien being. This creature would now own you, would lock you up in its cave. It wouldn't hurt you, in fact it would even feed you, with disgusting slop that other dinosaurs said was supposedly good for humans. And because you only get one meal a day, you are so hungry that you wolf this slop down. "Hunger forces it in, disgust forces it down" could be your motto. Thus strengthened (he must have liked it, after all he ate the whole thing), obviously you will get the same revolting slop every day. "That's obviously what he likes to eat!" they say. But you long to get your junk food back!

You vegetate in its cave day in, day out, sometimes you ask yourself what's the purpose of all of this, until one day you realize that it isn't intended to be cruel, no, just for fun. And because fun is how it's supposed to be (for the dinosaur anyway), you simply have to go along with it. It sucks to be the weaker one. Measures have been taken to prevent any chance of escape, and they have no qualms about even drastic measures such as castration. You will never see another human being again in your life, and when spoken to about this by other dinosaurs with less egotistical views, your dinosaur master justifies himself to his friends by saying "He doesn't know any different," or "He's grown accustomed to it." Is that not horrible? A being is condemned to life-long solitary confinement and they think he's doing fine because he **doesn't know any different** or because **he has gotten used to it**? If someone were to ask me what I thought hell was like, I'd pick this scenario. But the dinosaur tells his friends that he is a human lover, and that obviously he knows exactly what humans need, what is good for them, what food they like and what is healthy for them. And if he is an exceptional human lover, then he has read at least one book on humans written by another dinosaur who also obviously knows precisely how humans think and feel. Could it be that a dinosaur can **never** fathom the soul of a human being and truly know how humans think, what they feel, and what is good for them? Even less will a human being will ever be able to understand the soul of an animal.

Women don't even understand how men think and parents don't understand their children. Therefore how can anyone presume to know how an animal thinks and feels? There actually are, however, self-proclaimed animal psychologists who claim to know how a dog thinks and feels. And if you ask them how they know that, they will tell you that they've studied the behavior of dogs. The only problem with that is that they've studied the behavior of dogs in captivity. That would be just like deducing how humans behave from the behavior of convicts. Even those serving life sentences don't sit in jail all day long and cry. They too find ways to occupy themselves and sometimes laugh and sometimes feel joy, look forward to meals or going out for a walk in the prison yard. Well, now that you have learned that escape is impossible, you sit around and slowly become resigned to your fate. You actually no longer have any desire to break out. To come up with and carry out a daring escape plan, you'd not only have to be clever but also bold and prepared to take risks. In English and in German: it takes balls! But you no longer have any, and you lost your self-esteem, purpose for living, courage, and boldness along with them. You are tired, lazy, and listless, one day is just like any other. Every day is monotonously the same. Eventually you will no longer care what day or what year it is. Your "life" can described as "vegetating away" in the truest sense of the term. It no longer bothers you when your dinosaur master touches you. After all that is the only physical contact you get, even though the dinosaur is alien with his reptilian hide. Naturally you still have a latent hatred of your master, after all you know subconsciously that your master had you castrated. But for the most part you will suppress that. Because you are totally isolated from other humans, you will even begin to like your master, which obviously goes back to your very frail mental state. With abductions that last for long periods of time, this is known as "Stockholm Syndrome". It has been observed that in long-lasting abductions where the abductees are totally isolated, they start to identify with their abductors. This may even manifest itself as love for the abductor. Obviously this is nothing more than a subconscious psychological defense mechanism that has nothing to do with true, freely chosen love. It is a survival instinct, for if you were to always fight with and hate your master, he would soon have you put to sleep. So your survival instinct ensures that you act in such a way that will also enable you to survive, so that he lets you live!

Sometimes, when you have nothing to do, as always, images appear in your mind, images of freedom, images of love and strength. You won't know where these images come from, but they feel unbelievably good. They are images from your deepest subconscious, of your true nature. But you know that it is only a dream. When you get old and realize that the end is near, you will welcome the end and in death you will find the freedom that you were denied in life.

10. Species-Appropriate Animal Keeping

One must understand that the term species-appropriate animal keeping is itself meaningless drivel. Because nature never designed a single animal to be "kept". The basic principle of life is *freedom*!

If there even is a definition for it, or a DIN (German Institute for Standardization) standard, or any other claptrap dreamed up by German bureaucrats, it is most assuredly inadequate. You don't have to be a successor of Darwin or Alfred Brehms to see that many animals in zoos are kept in anything but a species-appropriate manner. Just think of the noble Siberian tiger, vegetating in its 4 x 4 meter [13 x 13 square-foot] cell, or bears or wolves. We cannot even begin to understand the ordeal that these animals are going through. Although such a zoo may have had a purpose in the DDR [German Democratic Republic], allowing an East German child to see an elephant even if he had no idea what a banana was, nowadays, in the era of DVDs and the World Wide Web, it is no longer comprehensible why one would allow a penguin that is used to double-digit negative temperatures and clean Antarctic saltwater to languish in stinking, stagnant water here in the summer where it hits 32 degrees Celsius [90 degrees Fahrenheit] in the shade. One *can let an animal live in the wild or one can keep it in captivity*, but one *cannot keep it in a species-appropriate manner*. One should not forget that the dungeon, prison, jail, the slammer, Sing Sing, or whatever else one may call it, is in all eras and in all cultures a punishment! And you are all debating whether an animal in a zoo is being kept in a species-appropriate manner? This animal is in the slammer, the dungeon! Frequently in solitary confinement in a very small space. What part of species-appropriate do you not understand? Why is deprivation of freedom used as a PUNISHMENT? Precisely because it is NOT species-appropriate! The fact that large animals in zoos rarely reproduce should be proof enough that these animals are suffering immeasurably and are totally depressed! I imagine that if a man and a woman were locked in a cell for ten months, assuredly two children would be conceived.

But if these two people were captured beforehand by strange beings and their wills, pride, and souls and thus their very essence were broken, and both of them were to sit there knowing that they would never get out alive, never see any other human beings again, in other words sit there in complete hopelessness and depression, with broken wills and broken hearts, then no children would see the light of day in there either. The fact that most [sexual] potency problems are mental in nature is no longer any secret. He wouldn't be able to get it up and she would subconsciously think: "Bring a child into this world? NEVER!" I don't know why zoologists have yet to realize this for themselves.

So what are zoos good for? So that people can see what an animal looks like? As I've already said, you can do that on DVDs or on the Web. Or go to the Natural History Museum in Berlin, at least those animals are no longer suffering. One should consider that from a purely ethical standpoint. Yes, I would submit that in principle any kind of animal keeping that serves to amuse us is far removed from any ethical behavior. Imagine that you were locked in a cage only four square meters [13 square feet] in area and these dinosaurs walked by and stared stupidly at you, some making dumb faces at you, others wanting to touch you. There you are, on exhibit for life, how would you feel? Yes, think long and hard about **how you would feel!** What is it good for? We surely cannot justify it with recreation, education, or culture, for then we could put people of other races, or those with handicaps, or felons on display so that school classes could see them live [and in person]. We could call that living biology or social studies. The mere suggestion of such a thing by a politician would be stigmatized as something from the darkest depths of Adolf Hitler's mind, and that politician's career would be over. Then what is it good for? Other than the fact that thousands of animals suffer in zoos and it costs the taxpayers millions. And even if someone comes up with a sensible answer to this question, is it worth locking up and torturing animals? When was the last time you went to the zoo? There you see completely neurotic and brain-deadened animals everywhere, animals who have been mentally violated and broken, many of them kept in solitary confinement. Especially pitiful are the predators, who ceaselessly pace back and forth in their narrow cages. Everyone knows deep down that this is cruelty, but no one does anything about it.

11. The Perversion of Breeding

Breeding could be understood as meaning that some of our contemporaries think they have to play God.

It is sad to see the results. Hard to believe that this subservient, trembling, pitiful thing in front of the supermarket was a proud wolf many generations ago. Some dogs can hardly walk, others can hardly breathe; they go through life gasping like someone with tuberculosis. The Germans have coined the term Qualzucht [breeding for defects] for this. I am of the opinion that any breeding is Qualzucht. Just look at certain breeds; it is pitiful. Legs that are much too short or too long, bulging eyes, incessant drooling, gasping, wheezing, behavior ranging from total subservience to extreme aggressiveness, just about everything that can make an animal suffer is represented. Such an animal is designed, just the way children build a sandcastle according to their own concepts, or a fashion designer designs clothing according to his concepts. The breeder likewise decides how the dog ought to look to fit the fashion standards of spoiled men and women. Welcome to Dr. Frankenstein's office! The breeder appears to give no thought to the fact that this is a living creature with a soul and basic natural-born rights. "Unconscionable" or "unethical" are just notions to them.

The spectrum ranges from dwarf breeds for spoiled women such as the Chihuahua, which weighs a mere 700 grams [1.5 pounds] or so, to the so-called giant breeds like the Great Dane or the Mastiff. Whereas the small breeds must struggle with everything from jaw problems to paralysis, including difficulty whelping [giving birth], the tendency to develop hydrocephaly [water on the brain], and slipped discs, the large breeds suffer from severe bone and joint disorders.

But size isn't the only breeding goal, there are also special extras such as the development of extreme skin folds in Shar-Pei that lead to chronic inflammations. In newborn puppies these folds sometimes develop into skin bulges that are so large that the puppies can no longer open their eyes. When that happens the skin is simply sewn to the head. Others like having a big ball of fluff on a leash and opt for a Hungarian Puli or Old English Sheepdog, which suffer extremely in hot weather. Those who breed and sell such dogs should be condemned to walk through the inner city in the hottest part of the summer, wearing a ski suit and a fur coat. Then perhaps they would see just what they are inflicting on these poor creatures. Then there are the so-called short-faced breeds like Pugs, Pekinese, or English Bulldogs, for whom difficulty breathing, bulging eyes, or difficulty swallowing are part of everyday life. One would think English Bulldogs were suffering from lifelong asthma attacks; do you think that constantly wheezing like that is fun for them? The massive skull in comparison to the rest of the body often makes normal birth impossible.

But it's not just appearance that matters, as we all know from our own searches for partners. If possible the personality should also fit. So it is simply bred in as well. Thus some small breeds are bred to be extremely dependent so that the glamour girl can feel that at least her little doggie loves her, even if she has no luck in her relationships with men. But it is not uncommon for these breeding results to manifest themselves as neurotic disorders, which culminate in such dogs getting severe jitters, being high strung, salivating heavily and vomiting when they are left alone. When they are alone they quite literally "suffer like dogs." But when they are alone, their mistress can't see them either, so naturally she doesn't care whether her little darling is suffering or not. The few minutes of joy when she comes home lead her to assume that he has it darn good with her.

On the other hand there are of course dogs whose aggression traits are highly sought after and bred into them. Since the beginning of the new century, there have been more and more reports in the news about dogs attacking people. It has become fashionable for a loser with aggressive tendencies to get an attack dog in order to boost his poor self-esteem. But obviously nobody is thinking about the dog, who becomes even more isolated because of this aggression. Nor does anyone consider the fact that such breeding gave rise to the need for leashes and muzzles, adding further stress to the poor dog who is already suffering as it is. It is truly hard to believe what some breeders think of just to make more money. Then there are actually breed standards! If a puppy doesn't meet these breed standards, naturally it is killed. Hello Adolf! It's as if you were to kill your son because he doesn't have blue eyes. Therefore when you buy a purebred dog or purebred cat, you must live with the fact that at least four others were born and then killed while still in the proverbial cradle. Someone please explain to me why puppies are killed merely because their coat markings aren't exactly what some sadistic Joe Schmoe wants!

Animal Protection Law:

§17

Whoever:

1. kills a vertebrate animal without a legitimate reason...

shall be sentenced to up to three years imprisonment or fined.

Is the fact that the coat markings are not the way that they should be, according to what someone wrote in a book, a *legitimate* reason?

These breed standards also change, just like fashion styles. It would be boring indeed if a 1970s German shepherd looked the same as a 21st century one. Whereas back then the ideal German shepherd had a straight backline and upright hindquarters, nowadays it is fashionable for the backline to slope downwards at the rear, which goes hand in hand with strong angulation of the hindquarters, a so-called coupé. The fact that this leads to unnatural stress on the joints doesn't matter to the owner, as long as the design is right. And obviously the breeder could care even less, as long as the designer dog fetches a good price. There is also a rabbit breed in which the ears span as much as 65 cm [2 feet], whereas the length of the animal's body is a mere 15 cm [6 inches]. Then there are Japanese waltzing mice, whose trembling circular movements could be interpreted as dancing with a stretch of the imagination, but in reality are merely a genetic defect, and Angora hamsters, who are incapable of grooming their extremely long fur themselves. This list could be continued ad infinitum. *These animals cannot survive on their own!!* Nature is perfect, and one cannot simply change something in it without making it worse. Human beings arose from nature and are not superior to it! Hence it is impossible for a human to top nature. There are still so many natural processes that we humans don't even begin to understand. Such nonsense as a lop-eared rabbit that constantly trips over its long ears would never arise naturally. Such a creature would never survive in the wild!

It would take extreme intellectual and moral callousness to breed or even buy something like that. At this point let us once again imagine our masters, the large dinosaurs, doing something like that to us. The result would be a cabinet of curiosities, a freak show of inconceivable dimensions. We would have drooling people with droopy facial features, extreme dwarfs, extreme giants, people with fur, crippled limbs, sickly wheezing hydrocephalics [people with extremely large heads due to water on the brain], bulging eyes, huge ears, extremely long or extremely short limbs, spotted coats like cows, some as aggressive as if they were on crack, others totally torpid, etc., etc. This would be a gallery of the most bizarre mutations of the true human race, which would fill us with pity, horror, disgust, and rage. If your newborn son was supposed to have a coat like a cow, but didn't, he would be drowned in a bucket of water right away. Because there are books personally recommended by "Adolfosaurus" himself that state quite specifically what this breed should look like. And after all what can the "Nazisaurus" do about the fact that your son doesn't look the way he's supposed to according to the Breeders' Bible? What if they bred humans who were no longer capable of surviving on their own because they were simply incapable of feeding themselves without outside help? These humans could do nothing more than live in homes where they had someone to look after them and feed them. If you were somehow able to stand up to the dinosaur, in the name of justice you would have to become a murderer. And no one would blame you if you did "Frankensteinsaurus" in! You would be hailed as a hero and go down in history if you freed us from these dinosaur monsters. But this is only fiction, in reality we are these monsters that commit crimes against other living creatures.

12. Soul-Crushing Dressage

In the past there may have been a need to train animals. Back then there was no entertainment industry, and the car had not been invented yet. Obviously it seemed reasonable to catch a horse and train it, and then keep it as a slave for the rest of its life. That was simply practical and a part of human evolution. But in our times, where a horse can be considerably more expensive than a car and where there are limitless entertainment options, why are animals still being trained at all? On one hand lies the inability of some people to change with the times ("My granddad trained animals in the circus, so I will too,") and on the other hand the fact that some people simply enjoy subjugating and tormenting other creatures. In these liberated times it is obviously a lot more difficult to treat one's wife that way in our culture. In most cases it is the man who is worried about his own equality. And if one can pursue one's perverse desires in the guise of sports or entertainment, so much the better. It is unfathomable how a person who tortures small animals is despised by his fellow humans, whereas one who tortures large animals, such as a dressage rider or a circus animal trainer, is considered a star. Dressage riding truly should be banned. The animals undergo immeasurable torture all for the sake of a score. Pictures of dressage horses foaming at the mouth have been circulated around the world, as have reports of doped horses. Dear "athletes," if you want to dope yourselves that's your own business, but doping an animal just so you can win a medal is truly evil!

In the summer of 2009 I went to a riding and jumping competition in a small town just outside Berlin. It was horrible! The horse owners arrived with their horses, two horses in a horse trailer about two meters square [6.5 square feet]. The horses had just enough room to stand, and couldn't move at all. And the most unbelievable thing was that two hours after arrival the horses were still in their trailers, while the owners took the opportunity to stretch their legs, drink a beer and eat a hotdog. Nor was there any place where they could have let the animals out to run unattended. I really had to make an effort to keep my mouth shut and not tell those snobs what barbarians they were.

Personally I find dressage not only degrading and ignoble, but also destructive. It is the totalitarian domination of another individual that has the natural-born right to live in freedom and dignity perfected to a "T". With dressage I am destroying the identity of a creature and forcing it to execute poses, gestures, and behaviors that are totally unnatural for it. If someone did that to a prisoner, Amnesty International would surely be out in full force. If a husband did that to his wife in our culture, he would go down in history as the personification of a barbarian.

But if a trainer does that to his lions, he receives applause. Do you really believe that the lion jumps through a ring of fire because some bozo on the other side has a treat for him? Definitely not. The whip is cracked, and to the lion that is the clear signal that the next crack of the whip won't miss if he doesn't jump. He found that out hundreds of times during the training. He was forced to jump through this ring hundreds of times with whips and electric prods. All animals have a natural-born instinct to avoid fire. We humans can overcome our fears because we can think rationally. But the lion can't. In front of him is the ring of fire, of which he is very afraid, behind him is the whip or electric prod, which he has felt countless times and thus fears even more.

Everyone likes seeing elephants in the circus. A circus elephant is captured as a calf in Southeast Asia. It is not uncommon for the whole herd to be slaughtered in doing so and for only the young to be left alive, because they can be sold for a profit. Of course this is illegal, but in Africa who cares? Just about anything there is possible with a few dollar bills. The young animals are hauled off to a training ground. There begins the cruel torture of "breaking in" for these proud, freedom-loving creatures. Which means total domination by human beings. The young elephant is tied to a frame and stuck and beaten with an elephant hook. He is denied food and water. Such hellish torture can last as long as a week until the elephant is compelled by fear, pain, hunger and thirst to give up and submit. People should think about that next time they see an elephant in the circus. In the wild African elephants live on the average of 56 years, whereas those born in captivity barely live 16.9 years. The British Royal Society for the Protection of Animals (RSPCA) found that out when they examined data on a total of 1,877 African elephants in European zoos and from Kenya's Amboseli National Park. This fact alone should be enough for a total ban, with no exceptions, on keeping wild animals for show.

You who go to the circus, do you even know that the animals are suffering for your sake? If you didn't pay for it, there would be no reason to torment these poor creatures any more. Do you go because of your children? If you told them how these animals *are compelled with beatings and torture to perform these acts*, then your children would likely be devastated, have nightmares, and voluntary steer clear of any circus.

13. Cats

Can you conceive of the fact that an animal comes into the world with an instinct and a plan to go along with it?? Nature herself designed that plan! It doesn't take a genius to see that nature is absolutely perfect, in fact infallible. Just look at the universe, countless heavenly bodies that are more accurate than a Swiss watch mechanism. Consider the perfect cycle of life, the self-purifying water cycle. Consider the miracle of the human being, a perfect, independently-thinking and -acting entity, with a self-healing mechanism. Capable of adapting to any environmental situation. Could you conceive of a car being made stronger through heavy stress? Imagine starting out in a 55 horsepower VW Polo and due to the long, hard journey, coming back with a Porsche 500 PS Bi Turbo. Imagine your car repairing itself, scratches in the paint disappearing. Even more severe damage like broken axles repairing themselves. Imagine your car running out of gas and then consuming non-essential parts of itself in order to keep on going when there is no service station for miles around. For instance, imagine that it could convert the back seat into gas. And when you do fill up again, you put in a few more liters and a new back seat appears. Obviously this sounds like nothing but a fairy tale, but that is **precisely** what every single living thing on this planet is able to do. Even lowly insects are perfect and autonomous. Airplanes are always crashing, but have you ever heard in the news about a fly crashing? That its wings simply failed? No, of course not, it would notice if it needed to rest its wings and would land. And what's more it needs no landing strip, it can land anywhere with no trouble, on the ground, perpendicularly on the wall, or even upside down on the ceiling. Or have you ever woken up with a total failure of your limbs, which was then fixed with a quick repair? The human body consists of around 70 billion cells, of which a few million are rejected and rebuilt every day. In this respect we get a completely renovated body about every seven years. The old is continuously being rejected, rebuilt, regenerated, and adapted. I want to get across to you that nature is absolutely perfect and has the perfect plan. Naturally she also has it for the "use" of her creations.

The plan for a cat is TO BE FREE! To have a territory, to hunt, to reproduce, to raise its young. A cat is a predator; that is its true purpose. When we neuter/spay a cat and put it in solitary confinement, we are doing the absolute worst thing that can be done to a living being: we are robbing it of the life nature intended it to have. With violence and mutilation, we are forcing a life on this animal that we envisioned, as if it were a commodity to do with as we please rather than a creature with a sensitive soul. What doesn't fit is made to fit! What purpose does it have for living now? Nothing to look forward to but getting up and wandering aimlessly through an apartment, boredom, and canned food!

The cat in your apartment no longer has any purpose in life!

It no longer knows itself why and for what purpose it's alive. You need to realize on no uncertain terms that what you are actually doing is worse than murder! This is an act of murder that will last the entire life of this poor cat and you refuse to see it. That is so perverted that there are no words to describe it. And you truly believe that you are an animal lover? You are prison guard and torturer rolled up in one. If someone did that to a human being, it would be called psychological torture (except for the castration, which is true torture = maiming).

When a cat lives on a farm, then it can do all that it was born to do. It has its territory, it can hunt mice, reproduce, defend its territory and its young. Obviously the farm isn't perfect either, for any of the following could happen: the farmer may drown its young, or most of them anyway, in a bucket or dash them against the wall. Now I'm talking to all of you women... imagine that you had twins and were very happy... then along comes your master and drowns your second-born child right before your eyes or simply dashes it against the wall. Because he heard that second-born children aren't very intelligent, or perhaps he drowns them both simply because there are enough already. Afterwards he pats you. And he tells his friends what a big human lover he is... such measures are simply necessary, he says. Sure! Because obviously Farmer Bill is very clever and knows exactly what's right or wrong.

Well, most cats don't live on farms where they "only" have to see their young get killed. Most live confined in apartments, where they don't even get a chance to have young.

And then the tomcat is housebroken, in other words, from now on he must pee like a human... What if this strange, giant creature were to force you to pee the way it did, i.e., in each corner to mark territory. And if you didn't, this creature would use harsh training measures to set you straight.

You would then sit on your rock alone all day as a eunuch, you would pee and poop like a strange creature, you would be totally catatonic, once a day you would be given absolutely revolting slop to eat. Truly exciting prospects for a young man who someday hoped to have a family and make something out of himself in life, no?

14. Dogs

Just like the cat, the wolf is also a predator.

A wolf is a pack animal that wants to live in freedom. This can be observed in wild wolves. There is a breeding pair that forms a pack with its young from the previous year and its young from this year. The older pair are the leaders and the young obey them without fighting. Such a wolf pack has between six and ten "members," who are in most cases a true family. When they become sexually mature after two years, they wander off and start their own pack somewhere. As one can see, a lot like us humans. Except that for most people sexual maturity comes a few weeks later.

What we said about dressage earlier obviously also applies to dog training. The only difference is that we're not talking about a few that live in a circus, but about millions living in German households.

I still fail to see what the dog owner gets out of the dog doing just what master wants. Master could just as easily take a remote-controlled car out for a walk, the car does everything that Master wants with no fuss. But because Master doesn't have to dominate the car like his dog and because the car doesn't look up to him in awe, he doesn't get the same dopamine rush with the car that he does with his dog. A father who did that to his son would be treated with utter contempt by his fellow human beings.

But if a person does that to his dog, it's called training and obviously it is good (for the person), because now the dog is a dog that will always assume whatever position its master tells it to. I have never understood why it is so terribly important for a master to know that his dog is waiting for him in front of the supermarket in a certain position.

You were not born so that some sack of crap could put you on a leash whenever he wants and tell you where you can pee... and if perchance your life really is like that, then at least you made that choice yourself!

Now let us once more briefly close our eyes and enter our imaginary cave.... The Tyrannosaurus rex, for some reason that we cannot fathom, wants us to assume certain positions at certain times. Everyone knows the feeling of not wanting to stand any longer and/or not wanting to sit any longer. During school you used to go to the bathroom even though you didn't really have to.

You are now tied up, while Master Rex goes out for a beer or is in the supermarket buying something. You were clearly commanded to sit or even lie down on the cold, dirty sidewalk. You are ruthlessly tugged home. You get yanked away if you catch the scent of another human, or even see one. If you are a somewhat stronger human, your dinosaur master considers buying a choke collar (so that he doesn't have to strain himself so while he subjugates you), which simply pulls tight around your neck if you don't go in the exact same direction as Master. You feel like you are being choked all the time. I don't find the comparison with waterboarding, which has been condemned worldwide, so farfetched.

If you are a well-trained human, then torture instruments like choke collars are obviously no longer needed because your will and your personal identity has long since been broken and now you are nothing more than a remote-controlled idiot with only one purpose: to compensate for a twisted creature's feelings of inferiority. If we are very well-trained humans that respond correctly at once to every word of our dinosaur masters and assume the correct position or pace or whatever, *in other words when our own will is suppressed to such an extent that it is no longer evident*, then Master Rex is proud of us. That's probably because he either can't afford a voice-controlled car or has no say anywhere else.

Obviously there is nothing worse for a social creature like a human being or a dog than isolation. Throughout history, solitary confinement and isolation from other human beings have been considered tools for torturing people, making them compliant, or punishing them. One might say isolation is the mother of all punishments! But this is precisely what is inflicted upon most dogs that live in German families! For all dogs in general, and for certain breeds in particular, it is torture to be left alone. While Master is flirting with his secretary all day, his compliant and dependent canine lady sits at home and waits and waits and waits and waits. Such a dog has nothing to do, cannot even turn on the TV or read a book, or call up her buddy. No, she lies around and waits and waits and waits until Master finally returns. The saying "suffer like a dog" wasn't just made up, it comes precisely from this suffering that dogs endure when they are alone. I had neighbors who had a small dog that howled for hours when they were both gone; it was truly heartbreaking. I used to wear headphones in my apartment so that I didn't have to listen to it. When I told my neighbors about it, they didn't believe me... actually I think it was more likely that they didn't want to believe it! To top it off, dogs do not have dog toilets. And why don't they? I believe it's because the smell would be too much. If a Chihuahua relieved itself on a tray with sand, the odor would likely still be bearable, but if a Great Dane crapped in your apartment it would smell pretty bad by the time you got home. "Of course I want a dog, they are so sweet!! ....What, you mean it has to go to the bathroom too? No, that won't do at all, not in my apartment. Where would I be if I had this stench in my apartment? He'll just have to hold it until I can take him out!"

Hence the poor dog has to wait ten hours until Master or Mistress returns. Imagine if a mother left her child alone at home for ten hours, locked the bathroom, and threatened the child with a severe punishment if he or she goes [poop] in the house. Once again I hear some smart-alec say, "But that's different." **No, it is not different!** Whether you're talking about a dog or a child, a full bladder is a full bladder. And fear of being punished is fear of being punished. It feels the same way for both of them, both have the same feelings, the only difference is that there is concern for one, but not the other. Only the human with his rational brain is capable of finding a solution. If he is a boy he can take a wizz out the window; a girl can do it in a container and dump it out the window. But the little dog has no alternative to this torture! Do that to your child and the child welfare agency will quickly decide that you are not fit to raise children. Do that to an animal and nobody cares. Or if you don't care about children, picture yourself back in your dinosaur cave and then imagine....

You have stagnant water, you're thirsty, but you don't want to drink because then you'd have to pee. And Master won't be home for another ten hours or so. So you learn to dehydrate yourself long enough to hold out until Master comes. But woe is you if he's a half an hour late, because by then you won't be able to hold it in anymore!

An animal is tortured with ten hours of loneliness just so Mommy can feel good for two minutes when she comes home and someone is glad. And perhaps the only reason he's glad is that now he can finally go out to pee.

Friederike Kempner wrote the following poem about loneliness:

Alone, alone, but not free,
Alone in a narrow cell –
Demons arise, wailing mournfully,
The only sound a scream; the only images, mad gestures.
Night – day – nothing – nothing – time stands still,
The heart is likewise still – quaking inside,
Outside – ice and death – inside it's alive,
Inside the human will boils and seethes.
The human will! Large and like the Furies,
Timid, weak! "Mercy," I beg:
"Throw me into the wild foaming sea,
I yearn for a quick death, not the living grave.
Oh, that human hands may push me off the jagged cliff!
Just let me see a single human face when you do –
Don't kill the sight – the sun still shines in heaven –
The deadened senses are gone forever!

I remember a convicts' revolt in England, where prisoners serving life sentences demanded the reinstatement of the death penalty because they felt that it would be more merciful than this dying by degrees.

15. Animal Protection Societies/Organizations

Animal protection societies or organizations by definition have the duty to protect animals. But do they really do so? I mean, TRULY?

Most animal protection societies are occupied with a wide variety of projects ranging from toad migrations to whaling, and last but not least, recurring topics such as livestock raising and in particular fur farms. Not long ago I had to listen to a pitch from an animal protection society soliciting donations out in front of a mall. It was about preserving the habitat of the orangutan. Obviously that is very commendable, but why don't these societies do something about cruelty to animals in their own country? That would be much more efficient, that would help a great many more animals. National awareness-raising campaigns could accomplish a great deal.

Nothing against the orangutans, they too should get to live in peace, but they have their freedom, they can mate and live the lives that nature intended for them, even though portions of "their" rainforests are being logged. But the guinea pig vegetating away in a plastic tub in some German child's room is in my opinion a lot more in need of outside help, for it too has its own personal Guantánamo. Why don't these organizations do anything about it? The answer is simple: because they don't dare! After all they are dependent upon donations from the same folks whom you just criticized for having cats. Obviously it's easy to go after a few moneybags who wear furs, and it's also easy to condemn meat producers and accuse them of being greedy for profits, for that you have the support of the masses behind you. Debates guided by envy have become very popular since Oskar Lafontaine. Were these organizations to tell the everyday citizens that what they wanted would cause meat prices to double at the very least, their popularity would assuredly suffer.

And it is precisely for this reason that they say nothing about millions of pets in Germany having to suffer and vegetate away under the most abominable conditions. But it's better not to tangle with the masses, even though there are breeders among them motivated purely by profit who keep breeding new dog and cat mutations that not only look odd but are also barely able to survive. At least there are some animal rights societies that do go after circuses. In this respect the European Animal and Environmental Protection Association (ETN by its German initials) and PETA are particularly worthy of praise. I would bet that if every animal protection society were to work together, thay would have long since succeeded in stopping the training and showing of wild animals in circuses. But each one has its own agenda. I wonder if there is any purpose at all in protesting the loss of species in other countries when millions of animals are being mutilated in our own country. One should get one's own house in order first. Especially since in one's own country such campaigns cost a lot less, it's a lot easier to be heard and understood, and a lot more gets accomplished as a result. Seriously, who in Sumatra cares about signatures being collected for a petition in Germany? So, dear animal rights activists, just join hands and work together on the greatest and noblest animal protection project of all time. Do justice to the name "animal rights activist" and don't worry about what other people say, but let your conscience be your guide. Millions of animals will thank you for it, you can step out of the shadows and accomplish great things.

16. The Ultimate In Animal Cruelty Has a Name: The Circus

In Germany there are currently more than 200 circuses that have exotic animals. It is no secret that the majority of these enterprises are teetering on the verge of bankruptcy. Obviously this means even more suffering for the animals, because they cut corners on expensive veterinarians and naturally also on feed.

It truly puzzles me why a circus, which travels from town to town and can never provide species-appropriate housing, is still allowed to keep lions, camels, or bears. They even have giraffes and hippopotamuses. Animals in the circus perform movements that are completely unnatural for animals, so-called "acts". If a person learns to walk on his hands, he does so of his own volition. But if a father were to force his son to do that using the carrot and stick principle, he would be treated with contempt. Even if he didn't use the whip, it would still be contemptible if he only gave his son love and rewards when the latter lived up to his bizarre expectations. Why aren't circuses simply banned? After all, fewer and fewer people go to them anyway. Today there are things that are a lot more entertaining than camels running in circles and a clown whom adults laugh at, rather than with.

And because fewer and fewer people are going to circuses, they take in less and less money and as a result it's once again the animals that suffer.

Do you know how a dancing bear learns to dance? When he's still a cub, he's locked in a small cage and a fire is made under the floor of it. So that the tender soles of his feet don't burn, he hops from one foot to another, which could be interpreted as dancing. A certain type of music is played while this is going on. The animal lovers of the circus repeat this torture so much that the cub is conditioned to "dance" when he hears the music because he automatically associates it with pain. Dancing bears have since been banned in Germany. But this procedure alone proves that animal trainers are cowardly sadists who will stop at nothing. Anyone who has any feeling whatsoever for animals would feel pity for such a young animal! But circus owners and workers are apparently completely emotionless, desensitized, sadistic, and brutish. An animal is subjected to torture and cruelty until it does exactly what they want it to do. I can assure you that if the types of training and the methods of the trainers were shown to the public under the big top, and if they were shown how these animals live behind the scenes, it would turn your stomach and your kids would start crying and have nightmares for months. It is cruel and barbaric. A circus animal spends 90% of its time in a cage that is much too small, in which some of them can't even turn around. During training they are beaten, harried, whipped, and given electric shocks to force them to perform maneuvers that are totally unnatural for any animal. Circuses are slave quarters and torture chambers rolled into one! Animal trainers are ruthless sadists whose only concern is to make money. It is truly reminiscent of the Dark Ages when people were still largely unenlightened.

Let us return once more to our stinking dinosaur cave scenario and imagine that we are living in their circus. By comparison their homes were like the Hilton, even though we did nothing there but sit around all day bored and catatonic, learned to do without water so we didn't have to pee, and eventually no longer noticed how revolting the slop really was. It was really no life at all, it was vegetating away. But we also knew that if we were somehow able to adjust, no one was going to do anything to us, in fact Master was even nice to us.

But now we are in the circus and Master Sadosaurus is the trainer. We live in a tiny 2 x 2 meter [6 x 6 foot] cell and the slop they feed us is worse than before. Just when we thought that it couldn't get any worse, now we see that nothing is impossible. Then along comes Master Sadosaurus, who yanks us out of our cage and teaches us manners. First he tortures us senselessly in order to teach us proper respect. Then he demands totally senseless things from us that humiliate us and cause us pain. We can discern no purpose in any of it and do it just to avoid pain. And it goes on day in, day out, with no end in sight. We hate every day that we wake up and pain, woe, and humiliation are our constant companions. We know that death is the only way out of this torture. Imagine such a life, wherein each new day brings more horrors, wherein each new day a sadistic brute comes and tortures you, and your suffering gives the spectators a thrill. You don't realize that the spectators don't want to hear anything about your suffering and see it as art; how could you know? You can't fathom what goes on in their heads any more than they can what goes on in yours. All you see is your pain and how it makes the crowd roar. Whereas before we sat in the cave completely catatonic and resigned to our fate, undoubtedly we would now wish for death. We would beg God to free us. Could this be why circus animals have the lowest life expectancy of all animals? Perhaps God heard their silent prayers. Galley slaves also had a very low life expectancy. Anyone who makes an earnest effort to put themselves in their place will see that this is absolutely the worst fate an animal can suffer. Once again I'd like to call on all animal protection societies to join forces in an initiative to deliver these animals from the hands of their tormenters. Every single animal trainer is violating the Animal Protection Act! And any halfway educated person knows this, not to mention every worker in an animal rights organization. So please, it's now up to you, otherwise you will never be able to convince anyone that you are truly interested in the welfare of our animals.

17. Hunting

Were you ever chased?

Perhaps you remember the feeling from when you were a little boy being chased by bigger boys who wanted to beat you up. Perhaps you know how it feels to be chased by a dog.

It is a terrible feeling. Even though the end of this encounter, should there be an encounter, is not fatal. In our civilized society at any rate, we cannot truly appreciate what animals experience when they are running for their lives because they are being pursued by a bloodthirsty barbarian with a gun and one or more dogs. The fact that people back in the Stone Age had to hunt to feed their families was completely normal, otherwise the human race would not have survived.

But why do people hunt nowadays? They say it's to maintain the balance of nature. I always thought that the balance of nature was maintained by nature itself, as the name says. Nor have I ever run across a red deer in the woods, so it can't be a question of overpopulation. Is hunting cruelty to animals? You better believe it! The animal is pursued and harried for a long period of time and finally shot. The animal can consider itself lucky if the first shot is instantly fatal. But that's rarely the case, so the pursuit of the wounded animal continues. The fact that the whole time the poor animal is scared to death and in great pain from the gunshot wound, often for hours, doesn't seem to bother the hunter much. At most he gets a feeling of power, something that he is denied in his everyday life. If these hunters really cared about nature, they should pick up the litter in German forests instead; that would be doing something worthwhile.

A few years ago I was in a pub where a hunting party was getting plastered. Make no mistake, just by looking at them you could tell what they were all about. And they were all feeling no pain, so it was no problem understanding every word spoken at that table.

There were 11 men between 30 and 45 years old. Eight of them were confirmed older bachelors. Three were married. The bachelors bragged about being single, not having a fat, dumb, nagging wife at home like the other three. The fact that there are also beautiful, slender, and loving wives evidently never entered their minds. Or more likely, they would simply never get wives like that. It wasn't hard to see that these were men who in their hunting and in their pub had the only things that made them feel like real men, from the look of them it was likely that even the volunteer fire company turned them down. What you really saw were 11 losers who bought themselves more manhood with their hunting licenses and guns. Cornering and shooting a defenseless jackrabbit evidently made them feel like John Rambo, or else it was one of those extremely rare moments when they got it up.

But what can the jackrabbit do about any of that? Furthermore, the jackrabbit also has natural enemies such as the fox, so no one needs to help nature out by shooting jackrabbits. And red deer are nearly extinct in Germany but still hunted under the guise of controlling the population. If that were true then hedgehogs should also be hunted, as they have no natural enemies. But nobody ever thought of hunting a hedgehog. That probably wouldn't be any fun for the hunters, because hedgehogs are very slow and curl up into a ball when threatened with danger. In other words a hedgehog is a party pooper. Bravo for Mr. Hedgehog! Besides a trophy like that mounted on the wall would look ridiculous. The upshot is that hunting serves to allow a few sadists to indulge their killer instincts without getting punished for it. Have you ever watched a deer through binoculars?

Have you ever looked into those beautiful soft brown eyes? That's exactly what a hunter sees through the scope on his gun. What kind of a barbarian would you have to be to see that and still be able to pull the trigger and destroy it? Who gives any thought to the pursued and senselessly murdered deer? Obviously nobody! What if our dinosaurs were to decide that our big cities were hopelessly overpopulated, and because humans no longer have any natural en-emies, a few particularly bloodthirsty dinosaurs with their shotguns had to help out? Obviously they are only doing it as a favor to us and the world! You leave your home suspecting nothing, and suddenly there is a giant creature 20 times your size and weight chasing your through the city. If after several hours it manages to corner you, it then guns you down without mercy. It doesn't care whether you have children or want to live. That evening in the pub it will boast about how it bagged you. It is 20 times bigger and stronger than you, it is armed and you're not. And it still brags about having killed you? Isn't that pitiful?

18. Birds

When was the last time you consciously watched birds in the wild? You can do that everywhere, in the woods, in a backyard garden, even in a city. You can actually feel how they enjoy their freedom, how sparrows tease each other, how they play with the wind as they fly, how they hop from branch to branch with absolute precision; one minute they're there, a few seconds later they are a hundred meters [100 yards] away. That is surely true freedom. "Free as a bird on the wing" is a common saying. Without much expense or effort, you can put up a birdhouse outside your window or on the balcony, or simply outside the kitchen window. This is a very good way to watch beautiful, free birds every day. It does the heart and soul good to watch these amusing and beautiful animals and how they enjoy their freedom. Please tell me, how did people ever get the idea to catch a free bird and put it in a small cage in which it can't fly at all? That is more cruel than words can express. Why would one do that? To enjoy looking at the bird? Wouldn't one have to be a sadist to enjoy watching a bird sitting in solitary confinement in a cage, totally depressed? Oh but of course, you put a mirror and a small plastic bird in his cage so that he doesn't feel so lonely. Why don't you just let him go, then he wouldn't feel lonely either? Oh, that's right, you want to stare at him every day.

Imagine yourself sitting in a cage in your dinosaur cave: you hardly have any room to move. The cage is so small that you cannot walk in it. Sometimes your dinosaur master comes right up to your cage and talks to you. His eyes are bigger than your head, his breath stinks so bad that it turns your stomach. He makes some noises that you cannot even interpret, let alone understand. But eventually, because you gradually become totally catatonic and less and less human, you simply begin to imitate these odd noises. Although it is merely a sure sign of your declining mental capacities, for Master Rex it is the ultimate revelation that he's doing everything right with his human. So that you don't feel so lonely, your master put a mirror and a small plastic doll that looks like a human in your cage. But certainly not the deluxe Beate Uhse [sex doll] model, oh no, just a store window mannequin. You will even kiss and pet this doll because your soul is crying out for love, for the love of another human being. Obviously this proves to your dinosaur master beyond a shadow of a doubt that you have it darn good! He brags to his friends at work what a great human lover he is. How well he understands how to keep you and how well he relates to you. "Mine even talks," he says. You gradually forget how to walk, your leg muscles atrophy and you are a total physical and mental wreck. Hope for a change for the better? You gave that up long ago. Your psyche is so badly damaged that you are no longer so sure that you even have one.

I would like to state that the provisions in our Animal Protection Act, if enforced, would suffice to ban keeping birds altogether. It doesn't take a genius to see that this is cruelty to animals. Flying is how a bird gets about. Yes, a bird can also walk, but we can also swim but that doesn't mean we live in pools. So if I confine a living creature in a small space where it can't move about as it normally does, then it shouldn't take a genius to realize that this is punishable under the Animal Protection Act.

But who really cares? Obviously not the bird breeder, because that's how he earns his living. The veterinarian? He too lives pretty well from tormented animals. That leaves the animal protection societies, who lack the courage to go against the masses, after all they depend on their donations. So when all is said and done, you could say that it is the loneliness of human beings and the greed of other human beings that lead to such intolerable circumstances. Does anyone think a politician has any interest in changing this? No, of course not, no politician would dare take on the public, because after all, parakeet owners are also voters. So in principle the politician isn't going to do anything like that if he wants to stay in power or acquire it. For the poor parakeets this is truly a dilemma. For them there is no way out!

19. Conclusion

This is a dilemma indeed:

The animal protection societies aren't willing (yet) to act, nor are the politicians (nor will they ever be).

And David? Well, he's just dumb enough to get half the nation mad at him. But perhaps he doesn't care what others think of him. Perhaps David simply cannot stand injustice. And oppressing, locking up, maiming, and isolating a weaker being is indisputably unjust. But maybe there are still some brave people in this country who will hear these words and not take the easy way out and ignore them, but who have the courage and the noble motivation to fight for justice for animals.

20. Frequently Heard Arguments For Having Pets

"They don't feel a thing when they are neutered."

It may be true that they don't feel the procedure itself, because (hopefully) they are under anesthesia. But if you are a man, you can certainly take the time and imagine someone doing that to you. OK, at first you don't realize what they are planning to do to you. Imagine you go out drinking with your friends, fall asleep, and wake up 100 grams [a fourth of a pound] lighter because your buddies decided to cut your testicles off. If you are a little annoyed afterwards, it could be that after all your testicles were important to you. But they tell you they did it for your own good.

You will never feel like a man again, your entire hormone balance collapses, a total nervous breakdown is imminent. If you are a woman, maybe you can imagine what it would mean to be sterile, never to be able to feel like a whole woman again and certainly not like a mother. Never able to have children. How much hatred would you feel if someone did this to you? I cannot imagine that anyone, male or female, would laugh it off.

"But my dog is doing fine!"

In all seriousness, how could you possibly know that? Did he tell you so himself? It may seem to you that he's doing fine, but any creature whose purpose in life has been taken away cannot truly be happy. Let us use a jail as a metaphor. An innocent young man is locked up in it. A life sentence of "preventive detention." He didn't do anything, he is completely innocent. Not a fighter by nature, instead he resigns himself to his fate rather than fighting to the death to obtain justice. He adapts to this life of confinement. He undoubtedly also experiences pleasurable moments, perhaps he likes certain television shows, or enjoys chatting with a certain fellow convict, likes playing cards, or certain books and visiting hours. Given the circumstances he is satisfied. But he is light years away from being *happy*. In his dreams he imagines what it would be like to have a family, touch his wife, be in love, have children, strive to advance professionally. Or maybe all he dreams of is having a fine-tuned car, breaking the speed limit, drinking and getting high and going to a brothel. Yet another dreams of travelling to exotic places, climbing lofty mountains, or diving on coral reefs. But *no free man dreams of sitting in jail playing cards and watching television.*

Yes, on the surface one could say, "He has it good: enough to eat every day, a warm bed, friends, and even television and books." A wolf living in the wild doesn't dream of getting castrated and sitting by himself in an apartment with his bladder about to burst waiting for his master for most of the day, either. So when you say that your dog has it good, that shows that you've never thought about nor chose to reflect on how such an animal would live in freedom, and that frankly you don't really care.

"He's long since gotten used to it."

That's similar to the previous example.

Obviously one gets accustomed to it, and this gradually turns into acceptance. But just because someone has grown accustomed to something bad does not mean by a long shot that they are happy. There are people who have lousy jobs, the work is dirty and grueling, the boss is a grouch, and the pay stinks. Nevertheless some stay in such jobs for the rest of their lives because they've gotten used to it. But people can escape from such situations if they really want to, after all they are not enslaved, in contrast to their pets.

"That's what dogs are for."

Okay, you may feel that way, but I bet if you asked your dog, he would convince you on no uncertain terms that the opposite is true.

Back before anyone had heard of women's liberation, the wife's place was in bed and in the kitchen, the husband was the boss and she had no rights. If someone today said that's what a woman is for, you would undoubtedly protest vehemently - if you are a woman! Many men, however, wish for those days to return. But those are not men with self-confidence, nor are they the successful, the strong, the intellectuals, or the just. Those are the failures who can't get anywhere in life and therefore need laws that enable them to dominate others. The same applies to racists! Nature never intended for any creature to live in captivity, that is purely a human invention. Our imaginary dinosaur masters could say the same thing, "That's what humans are for." Good luck!

"But others are a lot worse off."

True, you can always find a negative example if you want to. Every overweight woman has such an example: "Look at Hilde; compared to her I'm slender!"

The alcoholic says, "Just look at Tyler, he gets wasted every day." And that's just how every dog owner looks at the neighbor who is gone from home 11 hours every day and only takes his dog for a 7.5 minute walk. They all agree that "if *we* had to work such long hours, then we would never have gotten a dog." As if the extra 1.5 hours really make any difference. No animal kept in captivity deserves such a fate.

But small animals can't feel that.

Where did you come up with this baloney? How do you know that?

Have you ever seen the movie Horton Hears a Who?

Horton says: "A person's a person, no matter how small."

And furthermore, small by whose standards? In our dinosaur cave, it's we who are the small animals.

 "Oh, people! They are so small, they don't even feel it."

"But that's the way it's always been…"

…is something some smart-alec or other might say. A good answer to that would be: "Throughout history there have been things that were considered perfectly normal: slavery, oppressing other people, oppressing women, just to name a few." But times do change. And now it's time for our pets too to be allowed to live in dignity. And if it's "normal" for animals to suffer so, then we are barbarians! Anyone who thinks it's "normal" to maim or mutilate an animal is a barbarian!

"If I hadn't bought the cat, someone else would have."

That is a great excuse to soothe your conscience. Hired killers say the same thing! It works the same everywhere: supply and demand. If you hadn't bought that cat, that would have been one less demand. OK, that would be a mere drop in the bucket. But if a great many did the same, then fewer cats would be bred, plain and simple. As a consequence, fewer would be killed (because the breed markings weren't 100% correct) and fewer animals would suffer maiming and captivity. So take the first step and don't buy another pet when yours passes away, and get your friends to see your point of view. At this point some other smart-alec might say, "Then someday there would only be a few cats left." That may well be true, but better a few who are happy and living in freedom than millions in misery.

"In our culture it's normal to have animals."

In some ways that may be right, but why did we keep animals in the past? That was already explained in the beginning of this book. There are other cultures, for instance in some Islamic countries, that live under sharia law. Under sharia law, a woman may only leave the house when accompanied by her husband or her brother, she is not entitled to an education, does not have the right to vote, cannot choose her own husband - the father takes care of that - and the husband is officially allowed to mistreat her, in fact his right to do so is established by law. They call it "chastisement." If he wants to get rid of her, all he has to do is tell her three times that he's kicking her out, etc., etc.; the list of women's rights abuses in such regions goes on and on.

In our culture we are very much against that, except perhaps for a few wimps who only think they are men and would like things to be that way. But they are all losers who don't have any say at home, or can't even get a wife in the first place. But we do the exact same thing to our pets. Let's not forget: "Never torment an animal for fun, because they feel just like we do!"

"But MY dog loves me!"

That may be so, but why does he? I would like to point out that nature never intended for a dog to love a person. By observing nature, one can see that animals always seek the company of others of their kind. For example, you will never see a deer being friends with a jackrabbit, nor a squirrel hanging out with a fieldmouse. That is simply not the way nature intended things to be. As for your dog, he had no choice. Given the choice between freedom and his own kind or captivity and humans, any living creature would choose freedom and contact with its own kind. You would too, wouldn't you? If the dog still loves you anyway, it's only a survival mechanism known as

70

"Stockholm Syndrome." Even though you don't want to hear this, and think that it is honest and true love on your dog's part. Could you truly love your dinosaur master and would you prefer his company over that of other humans? The same is true for your dog.

"But animals have been bred to serve us."

It may seem that way to you because you don't know any different and it doesn't clash with your sense of justice and ethics. But in that case you should re-examine these two values very critically.

The following is very important:

Breeding can only strengthen traits that were already present to begin with. For example, dogs that are very small for their kind are crossed over and over, and their descendants get smaller and smaller. We have already seen how completely perverted that is. But because nature didn't give rise to any animal that likes living in servitude, this trait therefore cannot be strengthened. The animal must be dominated in order to keep it with us. There are no ifs, ands, or buts about it.

"My son loves riding ponies."

But he only enjoys it because you've never told him how cruel it is to the pony. Ask him how he would like having to walk around in a circle every day for 10-12 hours, carrying somebody else, or to be tied in a carousel and have to walk in a circle all day listening to dreadful music. If he knew that, then he would undoubtedly never want to participate in this kind of torture again!

"Aeons of love will be needed to pay off humanity's debt to the animals!"

- Christian Morgenstern

www.ingramcontent.com/pod-product-compliance
Lightning Source LLC
LaVergne TN
LVHW091208080426
835509LV00006B/899